CAROL AND JÜRGEN DIETHE

GHOSTS AT
THE GATE

POEMS AND STORIES

ISBN: 978-1-912270-11-8

CONTENTS

Ghosts at the Gate

GHOSTS AT THE GATE

Can we talk seriously now,
because the days are getting shorter
and the light more precious.

Another autumn is on the horizon,
the churning clockwork
turning full circle once again.

Let's speak about our hiding-places,
safe spaces when the wind howls,
halos of light when ghosts begin to gather.

Somewhere out there spells are intoned,
soups are bubbling when the rain is cold
and smiles are broken in lost faces.

We must talk seriously:
games are endgames,
and the referees are blind.

When you see the boat
navigating the black river
take your eyes off the boatman.

We've always known where it flows,
and the ghosts waiting at the gate
are clamouring to fetch us.

Hide when the wind howls,
don't listen to the voices
and cultivate the dying light.

CAROL DIETHE

TALES OF A HOUSE AND ITS WORLD

HOME SWEET TALK

Deanery Rondel

Words can never quite express
Its perfect *locus*, sense of space
And handsomely proportioned measure.
Room is found for every treasure;
Never full, the house invites
More furniture, more guests, more life.

The New Arrival is Quizzed

'Are you new? Ah, have you heard
Creaks or noises untoward?
Nothing? – Oh, they say your house
– Lovely though it is, of course –
Has a Poltergeist (all lies!)
Nobody could exorcise!
Nearly bought your house, you know!'
Over supper they debate
If I might be second rate?

The Deanery Would Like a Word

I grow old astride this cliff,
Paintwork thin and backbone stiff;
Solitary; dignified;
Rather stout – and vilified.

King-Sized

In the gully lay a nest;
In it lay an egg of vast
Dimension. And what happened then?
They Humpty-Dumptied it to cull
My progeny, the Dauphin gull.
I will avenge the murdered one;
Here on this chimney I will sit
And bomb those underneath with shit;
And play I-spy. For I can do
No other with a human foe,
Unarmed. (This last I hope to grow.)
I am the leader of the gang!
Thus the seagull monarch sang.

From the Visitors' Book

'Had a lovely stay!' they write,
'Did not see a single ghost!
Slept like logs throughout the night:
Darling, you are such a host!'

Deanery ad Infinitum

Age cannot wither me, nor time destroy
A particle of majesty
That I enjoy. My hour glass
Ticks the sandy hours;
And every grain is dear to me:
I hoard it into memory.

Scotland versus the World

Ici Londres, BBC!
Wo liegt Fortrose? By the sea?
What possessed you to migrate
To a land so cold and wet?
(Certainly a good address.)
World exchanged for – emptiness.

Deanery Farewell

My garden suffers from the shade.
The front is a truncated glade
Where canopies of three trees meet.
– With roots and tunnels at my feet
No wonder that I grow a-weary,
Long of wind and short of breath.
Mossy-roofed and window-bleary,
Ecumenical at best. Praying
Mainly to the summits, watching
Baby dolphins leap, I can
Conjure up the mermaids
And the company they keep. Death
Has stolen all my keepers,
Priest and laird and gentle folk;
Infants cried and widows weeded,
Soldiers ran from fire and smoke.
And I passed the time of century
With anyone who spoke. There are
Apples in the garden, and the sun
Dispels the gloom; there are roses
And forget-me-nots and lavender
In bloom. I can measure up to mountains
And I do not fear the Fall.
I shall stand here playing patience, safely
Closed within my wall,
Till, cathedralled like my neighbour,
Like a sentinel who must,
I shall genuflect, and topple,
And then crumble into dust.

THE HOUSEKEEPER'S ROOM

The boat had nearly landed; she was
Standing here, right by this window.
At that time the view was clear
Beyond the Firth towards the hills,
Before the church elbowed its way
Atop the cliff and stole the crown.
And nobody could save her son,
Helpless, she had to watch him drown.

My bedroom stores the mother's tears;
Her grief is unassuaged. I feel
Her haunting presence, and I try
To quell her pain.

The flowers in the room are fresh,
And yet the air stays musty, stale.
For she is trapped within these walls
And must remain

As though transfixed, and in a daze
I try to fight my fears. I know.
The prayers to lay her soul to rest
Were said in vain.

My children's balding teddy bears
Stand garrisoned beside my bed;
But there is mischief in the air
And spirits reign.

At dead of night, she tweaks me from

My sleep, and robs me of my dream.
I dimly sense her fleeting touch,
And her disdain.

BLACK ISLE

There are no fairies in the Fairy Glen,
Just muddy paths that give you feet of clay.
Across the water float the snowy peaks.
A pearly billow down the Great Glen streaks –
I smile to see that Inverness has rain.
Come with me, I will show you where
Those non-existent ghosts are said to tread.
Keep silent, though; we must not wake the dead.

No angels sit enthroned in Angel Court,
The Deanery could never boast a Dean,
No dryad nymphs protect the clootie tree.
Instead, it groans beneath the sweated weight
Of garments pinning hope on wizardry.
And in the Firth the dolphins twist and leap,
The air vibrates with silent dolphin sound.
And chattering skylarks hover all around.

A family of swans in strict formation
Glides into harbour hungry for its tea.
Do not believe the lore that swans portend
Calamity for fishermen at sea.
Now, shudder at the spot where witches burned,
And black hearts murderously spurned
The truthful prophet. Records are erased,
We all touch wood, and nobody is blamed.

Now Cromarty may well be 'fair to good',
But Meadow Bank has neither bank nor meadow,
The town of Fortrose never had a fort,
Though it was built in General Rose's shadow.

St. Boniface defaced, Cathedral Square
Soon fell to ruin, pillaged by the priests.
Where is the Bishop's palace now? The castle?
Yet echoes of the past chime everywhere.

I do not think my house is haunted now.
The footsteps in my mind are driven out
By other noise: for progress must progress,
Or so we tell ourselves. And houses sprout.
A bungalow by any other name
Would marshal field to conquer dell by stealth.
And hacienda blocks breeze down a lane
Where trees once danced in stately
commonwealth.

We wonder if the world will last, and how
We let it come to this. At night the stars,
White smudges in black ink, light the Black Isle,
And dawn bursts through the curtain all aglow.
Along the beach, we find Hugh Miller's trail,
And search for fossils near the caves. The wind,
Straight from the mountains, pounds our backs,
Lashing our spirits with another tale.

ÉCOSSAISE

When I become a Scot, I will
Cook dinner every day: on time;
And say mendaciously I love
The gardening. And I will take
Two shortbreads when invited out
To tea. And what needs manly strength
Will fall into the hands of my
Gemahl, a handyman of skill
As yet untried. And I shall be
The power behind the throne.

But will it be enough? Will it
Ever be enough? Would
Resistance not be better? Shall I
Burn my bra in public? Or storm
Parliament, perhaps? Shall I
Wear a G-string? Pack my bags
And seek a sunny shore? For
There must be something more!
Or have I failed to understand
A different rule of lore?

CULLODEN SCHOTTISCHE

The gale blasts through the woodland, raping trees.
They arch their backs to beg a mercy killing;
Skirts gathered under armpits, digits flailing,
A final pirouette, then on their knees
They fall exhausted by the battle done,
And whimper at a glimpse of watery sun.

The Highland mist envelops naked stumps.
A wall of rain becomes a winding sheet,
And prostrate trunks hear tell of other feet.
New shoots will sprout to put on dancing pumps,
But many a man died here far less entranced,
Shrieking in anguish at a jig not danced.

BURNS SUPPER

Who could wish for better weather?
Most of Scotland, as a rule.
New Year is an awful headache;
February – is cruel. So we
Hold a national ceilidh,
Gaily Gordon to the band,
Caper round as dashing sergeants
(Keep the whisky close to hand).
We will fight them on the beaches!
Slash the haggis, damn the English,
Clootie dumpling through the speeches –
Billets doux to Robbie Burns:
'The immortal memory!' A bard;
But not a feminist. – That said,
The lassies clearly loved him
When he tumbled them in bed.

SOUND WAVES AT ROSEMARKIE

The piper played a last lament
To mourn the tartan regiment.
A swim was only for the brave –
A choppy sea and breezy swell.
Because I'm deaf, I could not tell
The susurration of the wave,
And drag of shingle, turn of tide,
From gunfire at the Fort, astride
The southern tip of Moray Firth.
The sound played tricks along the beach;
The scattered sputter, out of reach
Of children playing in the surf,
Conveyed a sense of eerie gloom
That joyous sunny afternoon.
And God knows what the dolphins thought
Of training killers for the sport.

QUIET PLEASE, A MESSAGE FROM THE DOLPHINS

In the darkest depth of water
Dolphins weave through rusting hulks;
Sheets of plastic, banks of bottles,
Line the seabed. Past them skulks
A submarine. A dolphin sees
Or thinks he sees a tasty morsel,
Wrong again! Oh ladies, please!
Time to leave the water closet,
Head towards the ocean clean.
Rechts the Fort and links the golfers,
Shall we swim to Aberdeen?
Shall we let the Sutors woo us?
Shall we glide to Cromarty?
Nothing beats a good fish supper!
– Mammals need their energy.
All those planes disturb our rhythm,
Tell that Easyjet to land!
Let it disappear completely,
Leave us peace in sea and sand.

ORKNEY 4; EGYPT 0

How now, Maes Howe, do tell me how
Could Neolithic man discern
That shaft of light in chambered cairn,
Before the Viking hordes had swarmed,
Leaving graffiti, cuneiformed?

And tell me, pray, at Skara Brae,
How could they build that small estate
Of compact homes in stone and slate?
Who henged the mighty stones in place,
For Brodgar's Ring and for Stenness?

Amazing, how these feats were done,
Before the pyramids were born.

KINTAIL

On this pinnacle of high land,
I will slow down to a standstill.
I will watch out for the eagle,
While the deer bathe in the sun.
There is nothing I could wish for
With my family of sisters:
All five Amazons are standing,
Waiting for their saddled mount.
I shall wave to them, blow kisses;
And salute them as they beckon,
But I know they spell temptation
And I turn the other cheek,
So the sun can warm my shoulders
And the waterfall can speak.

BLACK SKYE

Inside the Disney world of Skye
We took a path to Snow White's Hills.
I lit a Hamlet (SMOKING KILLS –
So did the Prince of Denmark! –). Why?
What made us think we had the right
To walk towards those pointed peaks
That know a language no one speaks,
Except upon Walpurgis night?

We could not climb the gentlest scree.
Their steepled hats slightly askew
The Cuillins hatched a magic brew
Of cloud and mist and devilry.
Rebuffed, we dabbled in a pool,
And promised we would soon come back,
But will we ever find the track?
The ferns are rusting; nights are cool.

COLD MOUNTAINS

Sweet, sweet the icing on the cake
And pearly white as driven snow;
And frosted like great sugar mice
The hills in coats of ermine fleece
Now crouch in packs, as snug as ice,
Telling of gales, and winds that blow
Straight from the northern frozen lake.

The dying sun bids them goodnight
And bathes them rosy pink, to trick
Their melting hearts; oh, how they weep
And flush to feel the heated kiss,
Until the tingle turns to sleep.
But Jack be nimble, Jack be quick,
Come off the mountain while there's light.

CALEDONIAN SLEEPERS

At Morecambe Bay the danger signal flashed.
The engine stopped and everyone awoke.
A dozen souls quite intimate in sleep,
And fully dressed, felt naked and abashed;
Tested their limbs with caution, wondered how
They'd slept at all, bolt upright. Someone spoke:
"I thought these seats reclined." And now
We prayed for movement, dozed and counted
sheep.

The train catnaps at Morecambe, it would seem,
Restless, we sit and wait. Morecambe is wise:
We shall not pick the cockles in the bay.
What would we give to sleep, perchance to dream?
Rich as we are to travel on the train –
If only it would move. A woman sighs.
Not rich enough for berths, but can't complain.
Our carriage jolts; we lumber on our way.

And a blast from the past (1966)

ON BEING REGARDED AS A CAREER WOMAN ...

Live for your work, my dear,
Be proud of your post.
Be a worthy working wife,
Make your work your whole life –
Don't count the cost!

Why this long face, my dear?
Why all this strife?
Have you found the emptiness,
The loneliness, the strain and stress?
Then work for your life!

FIVE TABITHA STORIES

QUEEN TABITHA

Tabitha the ginger cat had been lying curled up on the sofa between the Grown-Ups, listening attentively to their conversation and at the same time pretending to be asleep, for what seemed ages. At last she stretched herself sleepily, yawned, jumped off the sofa and made her way to the door. "Miaow", she said expectantly. One of the Grown-Ups obediently got up to open the door for her, and she trotted out into the sunshine to the stream in the Green Wood, where she could sit and watch the fishes.

Swisket the squirrel, Red Setter and Horace Hedgehog were lying in the shade of Swisket's Old Oak Tree enjoying a quiet afternoon nap. Oohoo the owl was perched in the tree holding a heated conversation with Tomtit about whether it was better to sleep at night or by day.

"Hello", called Tabitha as loudly as she could.

Red Setter looked up and groaned. He had hoped for a peaceful afternoon away from Tabitha, and had crept out of the house when she wasn't looking to steal away into the Green Wood.

"Go away", he growled, "Can't you see we're all asleep?"

"Wake up!" commanded Tabitha, "I want to talk to you."

Swisket sat up and rubbed his eyes. "I was having such a lovely dream", he complained. "All about nuts."

Horace Hedgehog blinked himself awake. "What do you want to talk to us about?" he asked.

"Queens", declared Tabitha. "The Grown-Ups have just been telling me about their Queen."

Red Setter growled softly. "You mean you were listening in again whilst the Grown-Ups were talking", he protested.

"Hush!" said Tabitha, holding up a paw for effect. "The Queen is a very important person. I've decided that we need a queen in the Green Wood."

"What does the Queen do?" asked Swisket.

"She gives people good advice", Tabitha replied confidently, "and she eats banquets."

"What are banquets?" demanded Oohoo, who had swooped down to the ground so that he could hear better.

"I don't quite know", said Tabitha doubtfully, "but they must taste very nice."

"Where does the Queen live?" asked Horace Hedgehog.

"In a big house in London", Tabitha replied.

"Please Tabitha", began Tomtit shyly, "how far away is London?"

Tabitha looked very serious. She had no idea where London was, so she decided to invent an answer. "Ten times as far away as the stream is from the river", she replied.

The others exchanged significant glances. London must indeed be a very, very long way away.

"The Queen is very kind to people", Tabitha went on, "and of course, she's terribly brave." She looked round lazily and began to clean her whiskers. "Naturally", she added after a pause, "I would be willing to be your queen for a while. You could call me Queen Tabitha – or Queen Tab for short, if you like. It sounds rather nice." She repeated it over and over to herself with satisfaction. "Queen Tab, Queen Tab, Queen Tab …"

"What would you do if you were queen?" interrupted Swisket.

"I'd hold a court here in the mornings", Tabitha replied. "I'd solve all your problems for you and you would respect me, and do things for me."

"I don't think we need a queen", piped up Horace Hedgehog.

"No", agreed Red Setter, but he was cut short by the arrival of about a dozen nervous tits, who flapped into the clearing noisily, took shelter in the Old Oak Tree and began to squawk in terror.

"What's the matter?" Tabitha demanded, looking up into the branches.

Tomtit started to explain, "Please Tabitha …" he ventured.

"Queen Tabitha", she corrected.

Red Setter cocked his head to one side. Surely they had made it clear to Tabitha that they didn't *want* a queen. He looked at the others, but they were all staring up into the tree, so he decided not to say anything.

"Please, Queen Tabitha", Tomtit continued, "the tits say there are some bird-men in the Green Wood, and they're coming this way!"

"*Bird*-men?" repeated Tabitha.

"Yes", squeaked Tomtit in alarm. "They have two arms, two legs and birds' heads."

"Nonsense!" said Tabitha crossly.

"I'm scared", said Swisket, scrambling into his tree for shelter.

31

"So am I", declared Horace, shuffling away to hide behind his stone.

"Better not take any chances", said Oohoo, flying up to perch on the topmost branch of the Old Oak Tree.

Red Setter said nothing, but crept away silently to hide behind the holly bush.

Tabitha sat alone by the stream and carefully examined her claws. She was feeling just a tiny bit scared herself, but she wanted to show the others how brave she was. Suddenly there was a yelling and a shrieking, and six little boys dressed as Red Indians crashed into the clearing.

"*Now* we've got you!" shouted the leader, the feathers of his magnificent head dress swaying in the wind.

"Oh, *have* you?" cried another boy, retreating behind the Old Oak Tree. "Watch out for the tiger", yelled a third, pointing to Tabitha.

"Bang Bang!" shrieked the leader with the fine head dress, pointing his fingers at Tabitha. "Got her! Okay men, let's do a war dance!"

The boys behind the tree emerged, and a circle was formed in the clearing.

"Yahooh", yelled the leader, stamping round and brandishing a toy tomahawk.

"Yahooh", replied the others, joining in the dance.

"Me Big Chief Hokus-Pokus", shouted the leader.

"Big Chief Hokus-Pokus", chorused the others in reply.

Tabitha gazed at them, fascinated. She decided that it was much more entertaining than watching fishes.

At last the dance came to an end.

"Better go home", said the leader to the others, who immediately formed up in a line behind him.

"Yahooh!" he yelled and ran off in the direction he had come.

"Yahooh!" yelled his friends, hurrying to keep behind him. Within seconds they disappeared from the clearing, but the sounds of their retreat could be heard for some time afterwards. Gradually the cry of "yahooh" grew more and more distant, and silence at last returned to the Green Wood.

Horace Hedgehog emerged from behind his stone. "Did the bird-men hurt you, Queen Tab?" he asked, his eyes wide with awe.

"No, not really", Tabitha replied truthfully.

"You were very brave, Queen Tab", said Swisket, scrambling out of his tree.

"I know", she replied. "Queens always are."

"What's a tiger?" demanded Red Setter, coming out from behind his holly bush.

"A tiger is a big cat", Tabitha replied. "I suppose that means that I'm a small tiger", she added thoughtfully.

"Tabitha! Tabitha!" called a voice from the little house which could just be seen through the trees.

"O dear", said Tabitha, "what *do* the Grown-Ups want this time?" Nimbly she leapt over the stream, but stopped in her tracks to call back over her shoulder. "I'll hold court here tomorrow. Don't forget!"

Tabitha held court for a week. Every morning she marched into the clearing, and the tits immediately had to stop singing, in case she had something important to say. Oohoo had to keep awake in case he should miss anything, and Swisket was not allowed to attend to his store of nuts in case Tabitha needed him to run an errand for her. Horace Hedgehog had to sit still and listen carefully, because he was rather deaf, and it always annoyed Tabitha if she had to repeat anything. At last they could stand it no longer, and one morning, as they were sitting waiting for Tabitha to arrive, they held a conference.

"I must get some sleep", said Oohoo wearily.

"I must count my nuts", said Swisket.

Horace Hedgehog twitched his nose. "I've got an itch", he declared. "I can't *possibly* sit still this morning."

"I do wish we could sing", added Tomtit, and there was a twitter of agreement from the rest of the tits, perched expectantly in the branches.

But when Tabitha arrived, they did not dare to say anything. "Good morning, Queen Tab", they chorused.

"Good morning", she replied, settling herself in a comfortable position by the stream. Red Setter, her bodyguard, who had to follow her everywhere – at a respectful distance behind, of course – lay down a few yards away from her and prepared to go to sleep.

"I'm afraid I've got some bad news for you", Tabitha went on.

"What is it?" demanded Oohoo suspiciously.

"The Grown-Ups are taking me away on holiday", Tabitha replied.

"What's a holiday?" asked Swisket.

"A holiday is when the Grown-Ups put their clothes into boxes and take them with them to the sea."

"What's the sea?" asked Horace.

"The sea is a great, big, huge, *enormous* puddle of water where the river ends", explained Tabitha.

"Ooooooh!" squealed Horace Hedgehog. He had not realised that the world was quite so big.

Red Setter thumped his tail on the ground. His memory could just reach back to the previous year's holiday, when he had spent long happy laborious hours digging holes into the sand. "The Grown-Ups are taking me, too", he told the others proudly.

Tabitha ignored the interruption and looked round serenely.

"I'm afraid you'll be without a queen", she said. Nobody dared to say anything for fear of upsetting her.

"I do hope you'll be able to manage", she continued in a worried tone.

For one awful moment Swisket thought she was going to change her mind about the holiday, and stay with them. "I'm *sure* we'll be able to manage", he said hastily. "After all, we managed quite well before we knew about queens."

"Good", Tabitha purred. "Come along, Red Setter, we don't want to be left behind." Red Setter jumped to his feet, still wagging his tail at the thought of digging in the sand again, and the pair of them trotted out of the clearing.

"Thank *goodness*", squeaked Horace Hedgehog, hurrying away to deal with his itch.

"Hurray", hooted Oohoo, and flow off to his tree for a nice long sleep.

"Goodie goodie *goodie*", said Swisket, busily peering into his store-house in the tree-trunk to count his nuts.

Tomtit waited for a few moments to make sure that Tabitha was not coming back, and he told the tits that they could sing as much as they liked.

"Hurray for holidays", they warbled at the top of their voices, and soon Tomtit joined in the happy chant: "Goodbye to Queen Tab, goodbye to Queen Tab, goodbye, goodbye to Queen Tab!"

TABITHA'S PLAN

"Hello Swisket", said Red Setter as he stalked up to the spreading roots of the Old Oak Tree, where Swisket the squirrel was busy having breakfast.

"Have a nut?" asked Swisket by way of reply.

Red Setter looked at the pile of acorns with distaste and shook his head. "Have you heard?"

"Heard what?"

"Heard what the Grown-Ups are going to do."

"No."

Red Setter settled on his haunches and tried to look very important. "They're going to cut down Oohoo the owl's tree tomorrow."

Swisket looked at him in horror. "O dear", he said, and his voice was squeaky with excitement, "what will the Grown-Ups do next?"

"I don't know", replied Red Setter with a growl, "but if they cut down Oohoo's tree, nothing will be safe in the Green Wood any more." His eyes roved round the trees and bushes so that his words would have their full effect. Several blue tits had heard the conversation, and had stopped cheeping to listen. Horace Hedgehog emerged from underneath a holly bush and crept towards Red Setter so that he could hear better, because he was rather deaf.

"What shall we do?" asked Tabitha, the ginger cat. She and Red Setter lived in the same house, and they were not usually on speaking terms, but today was an exception.

"I didn't see *you* come", growled Red Setter.

"You weren't watching", purred Tabitha. "I followed you all the way here, and ..."

"What *are* we going to do?" interrupted Swisket nervously. "It's all right for you. *You* live in a house, but *I* live in a tree ..." He began to choke over the nut in his mouth, and Tabitha patted his back for him.

"Let's go and see Oohoo", said Red Setter. "We've got to make a plan."

"Wouldn't it be easier if Oohoo came to see us?" asked Tabitha, cleaning her whiskers. "Tomtit, be an angel and fetch him."

Tomtit flew off at once, because he was rather frightened of Tabitha, and in no time at all Oohoo swooped down and landed on Swiskit's neat pile of nuts, scattering them in all directions. Swisket looked rather hurt, but he knew that it must be very, very difficult to land exactly where one wanted to, and anyway, the Grown-Ups were going to cut down Oohoo's tree. So he didn't say anything.

"Well?" hooted Oohoo. "Has anyone got any ideas?" They all thought hard.

"I could bite the woodman", said Red Setter at length.

"I could peck him", said Oohoo.

"I could prick him", squeaked Horace.

"And Tabitha should scratch him", said Swisket.

"No No No *No*", said Tabitha crossly. "That wouldn't do at all. What if they sent *two* woodmen?"

They all fell silent, until Horace Hedgehog suddenly cried, "it wouldn't make any difference! I could prick them both!"

Red Setter began to laugh, and so did Swisket, until in the end everybody but Tabitha was rolling over with mirth. She waited for them to recover themselves, and then drew herself up to her full height.

"I've got a plan", she said importantly.

"Oh *do* tell us", pleaded Oohoo, fixing his big sad eyes on her.

"All right", she replied, examining her claws. Slowly she began to tell them her plan. It took a long time because she kept stopping to lick her paws. But nobody dared to say anything, because they all knew what Tabitha was like when she was in one of her moods. When she had finished, there was a hushed pause.

"Do you think it will work?" asked Oohoo at last, very seriously.

"Of course", snapped Tabitha. "I understand Grown-Ups."

"We shall have to be very brave", said Red Setter, glancing round at them. They all nodded gravely.

"It will work", said Swisket, happily selecting another nut. "It *must* work. We'll *make* it work."

The next day was a beautifully sunny day. The birds wanted to sing, but Tabitha had told them not to. So instead, they all flew to Oohoo's tree in silence and perched on the branches expectantly. Swisket was already there – he had come early to be sure of a comfortable position. Horace Hedgehog had stationed himself in a hollow provided by one of the big roots. Red Setter was lying in front of the tree. He looked as though he was asleep, but they all knew he wasn't – well, at least they *thought* they knew. Oohoo was right at the top of the tree, keeping a look-out. At last Tabitha strolled up, treading on Red Setter's tail as she went past, because she knew that would wake him up if he was asleep.

"You're late", he growled sulkily.

"No talking", she hissed, and leapt into one of the lower branches.

Suddenly Oohoo startled them all by giving a low hoot, the warning signal. There was the sound of twigs cracking underfoot, and finally two woodmen appeared. They put down their saw and gazed up at the tree.

"This must be the one", said the older man, whose name was Mr. Brown. He took a piece of paper from his pocket and looked at it. "The big horse chestnut tree standing in a clearing", he read out. "Yes, this is it all right."

"Isn't it quiet?" said the other man, who was Mr. Brown's son, Jim. Then he added, "We'd better get the dog out of the way." He whistled to Red Setter, but of course, Red Setter would not have moved for the world.

"He'll soon go when we start cutting", said Mr. Brown. "Let's get to work."

They put the saw into position, and Tabitha decided that the time had come to act.

"Go away", she miaowed, adding a hiss for good measure.

"Go away", twittered the birds.

"Go away", hooted Oohoo.

"What on earth's going on?" said Mr. Brown, shading his eyes and looking up into the branches. "This tree's full of animals."

Horace emerged from the shelter of his root and shouted at the top of his squeaky little voice, "go away!" Swisket jumped onto Tabitha's branch. "Go away", he shrilled. Red Setter got up and began to pace round the tree. "Go away", he barked. "Go away, go away."

For a few minutes the woodmen stood and looked at each other in bewilderment. Then Mr. Brown said to his son, "Let's go and fetch Mr. Jefferson." They put down the saw and marched away.

The birds started to sing jubilantly, but Tabitha called angrily to them to stop. "Didn't you hear what the men said?" she asked impatiently. Neither the birds nor Oohoo had heard anything: they had been too busy shouting. "They've gone to get Mr. Jefferson", Tabitha told them. Mr. Jefferson was the owner of the Green Wood, and they were all quite fond of him, but he was a Grown-Up, and of course there were *so* many things he didn't understand. The importance of Oohoo's tree was one of them.

About half an hour later, the sounds of people approaching were heard again, and Oohoo's tree became silent. The two woodmen appeared, followed by Mr. Jefferson and his daughter, a fair-haired little girl called Rachel who sometimes played in the Green Wood with her friends.

"I can't see anything wrong", said Mr. Jefferson, looking up at the tree.

"You wait", said Mr. Brown, nodding to Jim. They picked up the saw and put it into position again. At once Oohoo started to hoot loudly, and all the rest of the animals joined in. "Go away", they shouted. "Go away, go away!"

"Carry on", shouted Mr. Jefferson to the woodmen. "Take no notice of the birds, they're only scared."

Tabitha spat angrily. Scared indeed! What a typically silly Grown-Up thing to say. Red Setter circled the tree in desperation. "Go away", he growled, adding his voice to the din. "Go away, go away."

"Shall we carry on?" asked Mr. Brown doubtfully.

"Of course", replied Mr. Jefferson. He was feeling very cross, because he thought the woodmen were wasting his time. And then, quite suddenly, his daughter

Rachel sat down on a tuft of grass and began to cry loudly. The woodmen put down their saw and stared at her, and Oohoo hooted to the others to be quiet.

"What's the matter, Rachel?" asked Mr. Jefferson, completely forgetting that he was in a very bad temper.

The little girl pointed to the tree and howled. "I don't want the men to cut the tree down. *Please* don't let them cut the tree down."

"Why not?" asked her father.

"Because of the animals", she sobbed. "They look so pretty."

Tabitha snorted with disgust. Pretty! Pretty! Intelligent – yes, brave – yes – but *not* pretty! Swisket gave her a nudge and whispered "Shhhh! …" Red Setter was dying to go and lick the wonderful little girl who had called him pretty, but he thought he had better not, and gazed at her adoringly, wagging his tail, instead.

"Oh, all right", said Mr. Jefferson. "I suppose it doesn't *have* to come down." He picked Rachel up in his arms. "You can go home", he said to the woodmen, and strode off. Mr. Brown and his son followed him, carrying the heavy saw between them. Soon the Green Wood was quiet again. The Grown-Ups had gone.

Tabitha jumped to the ground and stretched herself in the sun, and Swisket ran down the tree trunk to join her. Oohoo swooped to the lowest branch and puffed his chest out happily. Horace Hedgehog remained where he was, because he had an itch, and was rubbing his back against the root trying to get rid of it. Red Setter was still wagging his tail. The little girl had called him pretty, he had heard it quite distinctly – well, she had said "they", but that included him, too.

"You're a genius", said Oohoo to Tabitha.

"I know", she replied sleepily.

"May we sing now?" asked Tomtit, very politely.

"Of course", Tabitha purred.

The birds began to warble with delight, and the others could not help but join in. All, that is, except Tabitha. She got up slowly and deliberately and started to walk away.

"Where are you going?" shouted Swisket in his high-pitched little voice.

"Home", she replied serenely. "I'm going home for a nap. Clever people need a lot of sleep." She gave a little purr of satisfaction, and disappeared into the bushes.

TABITHA TO THE RESCUE

Oohoo the Owl was perched on the topmost branch of his spreading Horse Chestnut tree, contemplating the big yellow moon and trying to decide whether the man in the moon was smiling or not. It was a calm, peaceful summer night in the Green Wood, the stars were twinkling brightly, and Oohoo was enjoying the beauty and silence which surrounded him. But the quiet was soon disturbed by the flapping of wings, and Tomtit flew up to Oohoo's perch and began to twitter nervously. Oohoo was not in the mood for company.

"What's the matter?" he asked crossly. "Pull yourself together and tell me what has frightened you." He glared at Tomtit, and then added in an undertone, "otherwise go away."

"O dear!" stammered Tomtit, trembling all over. "You'll never guess. Something awful – in fact, terrible …."

"What?" demanded Oohoo impatiently.

"Smoke!" Tomtit managed to stutter. "There's a fire in the Green Wood!"

Oohoo forgot his bad temper in a flash. "Where is it?" he asked anxiously, wishing that Tabitha the ginger cat were there. *She* would know what to do.

"Near the silver birch tree", Tomtit replied. "The bracken is on fire, and so are some of the bushes."

"We must go and warn Swisket", said Oohoo gravely. "The wind could easily spread the fire to the Old Oak Tree, and then Swisket *would* be in a mess. Come along!" and they flew off to the clearing by the stream to warn Swisket the Squirrel of the danger.

"Wake up! Wake up!" hooted Oohoo as they approached the Old Oak Tree and saw Swisket curled up fast asleep in one of the branches. "Danger! Fire! Wake up!"

Swisket sat up sleepily. "Fire?" he muttered. "Who said fire?"

"I did", said Oohoo, landing on Swisket's branch. He puffed his chest out importantly and told Swisket the dreadful news. Horace Hedgehog, woken by the noise, emerged from behind the stone and listened attentively. Then, without a word, he shuffled to the stream and stood with his little feet in the water, because someone had told him that fire could not possibly burn in water, and he was terrified that his fine, spiky prickles would catch fire.

"O my goodness!" gasped Swisket when he had heard all about the disaster. "What shall we do? My tree! My nuts! Oh, if only Tabitha were here!"

"Did anyone mention my name?" purred Tabitha as she strolled into the clearing. She had come to watch the fishes in the stream – they looked so much more interesting in the moonlight.

"Tabitha!" squealed Horace Hedgehog. He did not like her very much, but he knew how clever she was, so he was very, very relieved to see her. Perhaps she would know to put the fire out!

"Why aren't you at home in your basket?" Swisket asked in surprise. He remembered everything Tabitha had told him about the beautiful satin-lined basket in which she slept.

Tabitha half shut her eyes and stretched herself lazily. "I'm having a midnight prowl", she explained. Every self-respecting cat needs a midnight prowl now and then. It's such fun."

Oohoo nodded approvingly. He was rather partial to a midnight prowl himself. He never could understand why his friends chose to sleep during the night.

Tabitha put her nose in the air and sniffed. "Smoke!" she declared solemnly. "Smoke! And that means fire!"

"How can I protect my nuts?" Swisket asked worriedly, his eyes wide open in alarm. "I've got over a hundred nuts stored away in the tree trunk! What *shall* we do?"

Tabitha gazed up into the sky and saw the smoke billowing in the direction of the Old Oak Tree. The situation was very serious, but of course she could handle it. "Follow me!" she said to Swisket and Oohoo. "We'll go and wake the Grown-Ups."

Swisket and Tabitha hurried off to the little house which could just be seen through the trees, and Oohoo and Tomtit flew ahead of them, making as much noise as possible to warn the rest of the animals in the Green Wood of the danger. Horace Hedgehog laboriously waded through the stream and set off following Tabitha. He didn't see what use he would be, but he hated being left behind, and anyway, he didn't want to miss anything. When he arrived at the little red-brick house, the others were hard at work trying to wake Red Setter, who lived with Tabitha and the Grown-Ups and who was fast asleep in his basket behind the sofa in the living room. Swisket was tapping on the window, Tabitha was miaowing by the door, Oohoo was hooting loudly and Tomtit was chirping at the top of his voice. At last there was the sound of a soft growl from inside. Red Setter had woken up and was quite alarmed by the noise that was going on outside. He went to the door and snuffled vigorously.

Tabitha heard him and held up her paw as a signal for the others to stop. "Bark!" she commanded sharply through the door. "There's a fire in the Green Wood! We've got to wake the Grown-Ups!"

Red Setter sat back on his haunches, threw back his head and began to bark. He wanted Tabitha to be pleased with him, as for once they had been on quite good terms that day – Tabitha had only scolded him twice – and Red Setter had found it a very pleasant change. At last Mr. and Mrs. Benn, the Grown-Ups, woke up and came onto the landing. Mr. Benn switched on the light and shuffled downstairs in his bedroom slippers. Red Setter thumped his tail on the carpet and waited expectantly by the door.

"Whatever's the matter?" asked Mrs. Benn, as her husband opened the door and peered out into the darkness.

"It's Tabitha!" replied her husband crossly. "Naughty cat! Come inside at once!"

But Tabitha had no intention of going inside. "Miaow", she said politely, for she was never rude to the Grown-Ups.

Mr. Benn went onto the doorstep and took a deep breath of the cool night air. "That's funny", he said in a puzzled voice.

"What is?" demanded his wife from the landing.

"I can smell burning. Goodness gracious, the Green Wood is on fire. We must get a fire engine!"

Red Setter had slipped out of the door unnoticed and was wagging his tail, pleased to see all his friends. He did not care whether the Grown-Ups shut him out or not – he wanted to see what was going on.

"Let's go back to the Green Wood", suggested Tabitha when Mr. Benn had shut the door. "The Grown-Ups will soon put the fire out." So they all made their way to the clearing by the stream to await events.

For a while it did not look as though the Grown-Ups were going to fetch help in time. The animals clustered round the Old Oak Tree, listening to the crackling of the fire as it came closer and closer. And then, at last, there was a terrific clanging noise and a huge red monster with flashing eyes approached the scene.

"That's a fire engine", declared Tabitha to reassure her friends. She had never seen one before, but Mr. Benn had said he was going to get one, and he always did as he said.

Swisket retreated into the branches of his tree to do some mental arithmetic. "A hundred and seventeen nuts", he kept murmuring to himself. "A hundred and eighteen if you count the bad one."

Oohoo perched at the top of the tree and stared at the strange Grown-Ups with shiny yellow hats who poured out of the red monster. He wondered whether their hats were intended to look like the moon. He gazed up into sky reflectively and decided there was a definite resemblance.

Horace Hedgehog peeped from behind a root and watched with boggling eyes as the peculiar Grown-Ups held on to a huge, wriggly water snake. It must be a water snake, he concluded, because water was pouring out of it all the time. Or was it a fire snake, because it was putting the fire out? He would have liked to ask Tabitha, but she had turned her back on the scene and was gazing intently into the stream, watching the silver fishes in the inky water. Horace knew that it was better not to bother her when she was in one of her moods.

Red Setter stared at Mr. and Mrs. Benn with curiosity. They were standing arm in arm watching the fire, and to his limited knowledge they only stood like that when they were happy. But what was there to be happy about, when there was a fire in the Green Wood! He gave a little sigh and decided that he would never be able to understand the Grown-Ups like Tabitha did.

Tomtit was flying from tree to tree watching the firemen's progress, and giving little cheeps of delight as he saw the flames die down one by one. At length the sound of crackling ceased, the smoke disappeared, and there were no more flames to be seen. The only evidence of the fire was a cluster of wet, charred bushes and the stale smell of smoke which lingered in the air. The firemen wound the hose back onto their engine with obvious satisfaction, got inside the machine and drove off. But Mr. and Mrs. Benn stayed by the stream for some time, arm in arm, and there was a long silence. At last Mrs. Benn spoke. "I suppose we'd better go home", she said, turning round. "Thank goodness Tabitha raised the alarm!"

Tabitha purred softly and looked round to make sure that her friends had heard the compliment.

"Well done, Tabitha", hooted Oohoo.

"Yes", ventured Tomtit reluctantly. He had just remembered that he didn't like Tabitha very much.

"A hundred and seventeen", said Swisket absent-mindedly.

Red Setter's heart sank. Why did the Grown-Ups always praise Tabitha? Hadn't he barked till his throat was sore?

Mr. Benn whistled, and Red Setter got up obediently and trotted over to him. "You're a clever dog, too, aren't you, barking like that?" said Mr. Benn, stroking Red Setter's head. Red Setter nearly wagged his tail off with delight. At last, at long, long last, the Grown-Ups realised his true worth! For one fleeting moment he was almost glad there had been a fire in the Green Wood.

Mr. and Mrs. Benn set off to their house, and Tabitha and Red Setter followed them at a distance, their heads held proudly. Together they had saved the Green Wood! Soon the lights of the little house went out, and the only illumination in the Green Wood was the moon.

"I'm going back to my tree", said Oohoo, and flew away briskly.

"I'll come too", said Tomtit. He liked to sleep in the lower branches of Oohoo's Horse Chestnut tree.

Horace Hedgehog ambled over to his stone and settled himself down comfortably. "Goodnight", he called to Swisket, who was still crouching on his branch in the Old Oak Tree, deep in thought.

"A hundred and seventeen", Swisket replied wearily. "No, a hundred and eighteen …. anyway", he added, "the fire has been put out." He curled up into a soft, fluffy little ball and fell fast asleep.

TABITHA TRIES TO TEACH

"Don't you think that Tabitha's frightfully clever?" Swisket Squirrel asked Red Setter thoughtfully. They were sitting in the shade of the Old Oak Tree beside the stream, watching the fishes and enjoying the sunshine. Red Setter paused before he replied. It was his misfortune to live with Tabitha, the ginger cat, and he did not quite share Swisket's admiration of her; in fact, he and Tabitha had not been on speaking terms for a week. But he could not deny that she was clever – even frightfully clever.

"I suppose she is", he said at last, with the trace of a growl.

Oohoo the Owl, who was perched on one of the lower branches of the Old Oak Tree, had overheard the conversation, and he swooped down to sit beside Swisket. "I think she's frightfully clever, too", he said.

"I don't like her very much, though", squeaked Horace Hedgehog. The others turned in surprise to see him sitting on a big flat stone beside the stream.

"How long have you been there?" asked Swisket.

"Ages", replied Horace rather sadly. "I've been sitting here for simply *ages* waiting for someone to notice me."

"Come over here", commanded Oohoo. "We're going to have a discussion." He waited for Horace to amble over, and then he puffed out his chest, as he always did when he was feeling pleased with himself. "I've invited Tabitha to come over here this afternoon", he said. "She's going to teach the tits a few lessons – you know how ignorant they are."

"Here?" repeated Swisket, "at my oak tree? Why here? Why not at your tree?"

Oohoo pointed to the stream with his wing. "You *know* how Tabitha loves to sit and watch the fishes", he said importantly. "And anyway, *we* might learn a thing or two as well." He winked at Red Setter, who immediately turned his back sulkily. He knew all he wished to know about Tabitha already.

Soon afterwards the tits began to arrive for their lessons. They were looking very clean and smart, because they wanted Tabitha to be pleased with them. They all perched in a row on the lowest branch of the Old Oak Tree, and waited expectantly for their teacher. At last Tabitha emerged from the bushes and surveyed the scene before her with satisfaction. She chose a comfortable spot by the stream and sat watching the fishes for several minutes in silence. In fact, she so far forgot herself as to dip her paw into the water.

"Tabitha!" shouted Oohoo rather crossly, "the tits are waiting for their lesson!"

"Of course", she purred. "What would you like me to teach them?"

Everyone was silent. They simply hadn't given the matter any thought. At last Tomtit plucked up the courage to say shyly, "Please Tabitha, will you teach us something about the Grown-Ups?"

She beamed happily. It was her very, very favourite subject — she knew all about the Grown-Ups. In fact, she *understood* them.

"They always have hair on their heads", she began, her green eyes twinkling in the sun, "and they all love animals."

"Do they love birds?" asked Tomtit anxiously.

"I suppose so", she replied, licking her paw.

"How can we *know*?" Tomtit insisted.

"Well, if they love you, they give you milk when you ask for it."

There was a hum of conversation. The tits all asked each other what milk was; Swisket asked Oohoo what it tasted like.

"Milk is white water which tastes nice", Tabitha said when the noise had quietened down.

"Please Tabitha", asked Tomtit nervously, "will you teach us how to ask for milk?"

"It's easy", she replied sweetly. "All you say is Miaow. You'd better repeat it after me: Miaow, Miaow."

"Tweet, tweet", twittered the birds obediently.

"No!" said Tabitha angrily. "You're not trying! Say Miaow!"

"Tweet."

"*Miaow.*"

"*Tweet.*"

Tabitha hissed and arched her back. "You're so stupid", she said, looking up at the birds, "that I could *eat* you."

There was a terrific fluttering of wings, and within seconds the tits had flown away in terror.

"O dear", said Oohoo, "you've frightened them. Now they'll never come back for another lesson."

"Maybe we could have a lesson instead", ventured Swisket. He wanted to hear more about the Grown-Ups.

"Tell us about the houses the Grown-Ups live in", begged Horace.

Tabitha made herself comfortable again and gazed up into the empty branches of the Old Oak Tree. "Houses are trees with lids on", she explained.

"Why lids?" asked Horace.

"Because Grown-Ups don't like getting wet", said Tabitha. "Even *I* know that."

"Inside the grass is very short and soft", Tabitha continued, ignoring the interruption.

"How soft?" demanded Oohoo.

"Almost as soft as my fur", replied Tabitha, holding out a paw for their inspection. "And lots of different colours – red, yellow, blue, pink ...."

"Oooooh!" squealed Horace excitedly. He was trying to imagine pink grass.

"They like to sit listening to little boxes which make squeaky noises", Tabitha went on, "and they have lots of yellow suns which light up after the real sun has gone to bed."

"Oooooh!" said Horace again.

"Isn't that right, Red Setter?" Tabitha asked sharply, because she could see that he was nearly asleep.

"Uhh – yes", replied Red Setter gruffly.

Just then the sky went very dark, and a few large drops of rain began to fall.

"O my goodness", said Tabitha. "I don't like getting wet either. Good-bye." And with that she leapt across the stream and made a dash for her house, which they could just see through the trees. Soon Red Setter got up and hurried after her.

"I'd *love* to see the pink grass", said Horace, sitting happily in a puddle while the rain drops splashed off him.

"I'd *love* to see the yellow suns", said Swisket.

Oohoo said nothing. He was wondering how long it would take him to persuade the tits that Tabitha wasn't going to eat them.

"Why don't we go and explore Tabitha's house", said Swisket suddenly.

"Good idea", squeaked Horace.

"Hmm", said Oohoo. "I don't know."

"Oh, come *on*", said Swisket eagerly.

So the three of them set off. Oohoo and Swisket had to keep stopping to wait for Horace Hedgehog, but at last they arrived at the doorstep of the little red-brick house. The door was wide open, so they marched straight in, and saw Tabitha curled up beside the fire.

"Tabitha!" called Swisket, "we've come to see the house!"

Tabitha looked at them in alarm. "O dear", she said, "the Grown-Ups won't be pleased at all! You'd better go away again quickly."

They turned to go, but the door was shut, and for a few moments they stood looking at Tabitha helplessly, the rain dripping off them and forming little puddles on the pink carpet.

"You'd better hide in Red Setter's basket", whispered Tabitha, and they climbed into the basket behind the sofa just in time. A few seconds later Tabitha's Grown-Ups, Mr. and Mrs. Benn, came in and turned on the radio to listen to the news. It began to grow dark, and Mr. Benn got up to put the lights on. Swisket, Oohoo and Horace crouched in the basket, thrilled by what they saw and heard. Swisket gazed up at the little yellow suns and wondered if they were hot, like the real sun. Horace sat and pondered whether or not he liked pink grass. Oohoo listened attentively to the voice speaking from the little box, and wondered how on earth a Grown-Up had ever managed to squeeze inside. Suddenly there was a scratching at the door, and Mrs. Benn got up to let

Red Setter in. He pattered into the room, wagged his tail at the Grown-Ups, and disappeared behind the sofa for a nap in his basket.

"Woof!" He sprang out again, howling with pain. "Grumph!" he barked to the Grown-Ups, trying to tell them that something had pricked him. "Woof!! Grumph!!"

"Hush!" hissed Tabitha. "It's only Horace's prickles!"

But it was too late. Mrs. Benn had got up to peep behind the sofa. "Goodness gracious!" she exclaimed. "There's a squirrel in the dog's basket. And a hedgehog. Oh – *and* an owl!"

Swisket scrambled out and ran up the tall lampshade to perch near the little yellow sun, but it was very hot, so he leapt onto the mantelpiece and sat there, trembling. Oohoo began to fly round the room to try to find a way out, but he kept upsetting things and made Mrs. Benn scream. Red Setter barked loudly, because he didn't understand what was going on. Tabitha took shelter under the table, and watched the scene calmly, while Horace Hedgehog laboriously made his way to the door and stationed himself beside it, patiently. At last Mr. Benn noticed him and hurried to open the door for him. So Horace shuffled out into the cool night air, followed by Oohoo, screeching angrily, and a few seconds later Swisket ran out to join them; and they retreated into the safety of the Green Wood to sit under the Old Oak Tree and talk about their adventure.

"I'd *much* rather have green grass", said Horace confidentially. "It smells sweeter."

"I'd *much* rather have the real sun", said Swisket. "Or the moon", he added, looking up into the sky.

"I'd *much* rather have a proper tree", hooted Oohoo. "A nice sensible tree with no lid on."

But the next day, when Tabitha asked them what they thought of her house, they replied that it was very, very interesting. Red Setter looked at them with curiosity. He didn't quite see how anyone could call the previous night's adventure interesting. As for him, he had found it perfectly terrifying, and Tabitha had given him a long lecture afterwards about his silly behaviour.

"What shall I teach you today?" asked Tabitha.

Swisket looked at Oohoo. Oohoo winked at Horace. Horace sidled up to Red Setter and cocked his head to one side. Red Setter decided that he had better say something. "I think you've taught them just about everything", he told Tabitha. "After all, they *have* been to see for themselves."

Tabitha looked rather disappointed. She liked being a teacher and having them all listen to her and ask her questions. "Oh, all right", she said, turning her back on them. "I expect you *enjoy* being stupid." And she peered into the stream to watch the fishes darting and jumping in the cool, clear water. The others nodded to each other, and one by one they slipped away into the bushes, leaving her alone with the fishes and her frightfully clever thoughts.

TABITHA HAS KITTENS

"Where's Tabitha?" Swisket Squirrel asked Oohoo the Owl one day when they were sitting in the lower branches of the Old Oak Tree, enjoying the sunshine and the gurgling of the stream below.

"I don't know", replied Oohoo. "I haven't seen her for ages." And then he called down to Red Setter, who was fast asleep in the shade of the Old Oak Tree. "Wake up, Red Setter! We want to know what's happened to Tabitha!"

Red Setter sat up sleepily. "Uh?" he grunted. "Tabitha? Oh – she's had some kittens." And he lay down again with a little growl in the hope of continuing his nap.

"Kittens!" squeaked Horace Hedgehog, emerging from behind his special stone. "How many kittens?"

"Four", replied Red Setter gruffly.

"Oooooh!!" squealed Horace. "What do they look like?" By this time Red Setter was fully awake. He stood up to shake himself, and then he sat back on his haunches and said dolefully, "they look just like Tabitha!" The prospect of the house being invaded by four more cats horrified him. It was bad enough having Tabitha to boss him around, but five of them! Why, it was just too awful to think about. And they were all ginger; that made it so much worse.

"What are their names?" persisted Horace.

"Petrinella, Mirabelle, Algernon and Bobs", recited Red Setter with a shudder.

"What funny names", said Horace thoughtfully, but was prevented from asking further questions by the arrival of Tabitha herself – and not the normal, sedate

Tabitha who usually marched into the clearing, but a nervous, trembling bundle of fur and whiskers.

"What's the matter, Tabitha?" hooted Oohoo.

"It's the Grown-Ups!" she replied. "They're going to take my kittens away!"

Horace's eyes went wide with amazement. "What will they do to them?"

"I don't know", replied Tabitha unhappily. "But I've heard the most dreadful stories from other cats."

Tomtit had flown into the clearing and was perched in the holly bush, listening attentively to the conversation. "Please Tabitha", he piped up shyly, "didn't you once say that all Grown-Ups love animals?"

Tabitha did not bother to reply. "Where can I hide my kittens?" she asked, helplessly staring round at the others.

Nobody spoke for a little while: they were all so surprised at seeing Tabitha in this state. At last Oohoo broke the silence. "How much room is there in the hollow of the tree trunk?" he asked Swisket sternly.

"No room at all", replied Swisket. "It's full of nuts, absolutely full to the brim. The kittens wouldn't fit in."

"You could hide the kittens behind my stone", Horace offered. He did not like Tabitha very much, but he felt sorry for her poor little kittens.

"What about here, in the shelter of this big root?" suggested Red Setter, scratching round the foot of the Old Oak Tree.

Tabitha went to examine the spot, and gave a little purr of approval. "I'll go and fetch my kittens at once", she said.

"I'll come and help you", said Red Setter, and they trolled away together. He and Tabitha were not usually on very good terms, but just this once he was prepared to go out of his way to help her, if it meant there would be fewer cats in the house. They made two journeys to and from the little red-brick house which could just be seen through the trees, carrying the kittens gently in their mouths, and at last the tiny creatures were safely installed in the hollow of the root of the Old Oak Tree.

"Who's going to look after my kittens when I'm not here?" demanded Tabitha, looking round expectantly.

"I'll keep an eye on them during the night", said Oohoo – rather reluctantly, because it meant that he would be away from his own tree. "After all, I never sleep at night."

"I'll help too", chimed in Tomtit. "I'm very good at warning people if anything goes wrong."

"And I'll look after them during the day", said Swisket. "That is, when I'm not busy counting my nuts."

"And I'll help him", said Horace eagerly, anxious not to be left out.

"Thank you", purred Tabitha. Just then a voice was heard calling "Tabitha!! Tabitha!" "O dear", she sighed, "I do hope the Grown-Ups haven't found out already." She looked at Swisket sharply. "Are you sure you know how to look after kittens?" she asked.

"I suppose they – er – don't eat nuts?" Swisket replied awkwardly.

Tabitha snorted with indignation. "That's a very silly question", she said crossly. "A squirrel of your age ought to know better."

"How old *am* I?" demanded Swisket, fascinated. He had no idea how old he was, and neither had Tabitha, so the subject was dropped.

"Tabitha!" called the voice again, and she reluctantly sprang over the stream and disappeared.

The kittens remained in the Green Wood for a whole week. Every day Tabitha came to make sure they were alright, and even Red Setter was quite interested to see them playing games with each other. Mirabelle and Petrinella were no trouble at all, although Petrinella did steal one of Swisket's nuts one day and used it as a ball, until a horrified Swisket managed to rescue it. Algernon was very weak, and Horace Hedgehog was quite concerned about him. Bobs kept trying to creep away, but Tomtit always spotted him before he got very far and cheeped loudly as a warning for the others to keep an eye on him. So a whole week went by: a busy week for the animals in the clearing in the Green Wood.

One day they were all in the clearing occupied in various ways. Mirabelle and Bobs were having an argument, Petrinalla was playing with a twig, and Algernon was having a sleep beside Tabitha, who was sitting by the stream so that she could watch her kittens and still have an occasional peep at the fishes darting in the cool, clear water. Tomtit was having forty winks in the Old Oak Tree because he had been awake for most of the night making sure that Bobs did not escape, and beside him was perched Oohoo – a very sleepy Oohoo who kept dozing off at intervals and snoring loudly. Swisket was counting his nuts. He now made a point of counting them all twice a day, to make sure that Petrinalla had not helped herself to another ball. Red Setter was digging for a bone he had buried some months ago, and Horace was protesting at the top of his squeaky little voice because Red Setter was sending earth all over his stone. There was such a general commotion that none of the little gathering heard the sound of footsteps approaching, and they were all taken by surprise when Tabitha's Grown-Ups, Mr. and Mrs. Benn, walked into the clearing arm in arm.

"Oh, look!" said Mrs. Benn. "There's Tabitha! And there are her kittens." She bent down and carefully picked up Mirabelle and Petrinella. "Thank goodness we've found them", she said to her husband. "Just fancy – we were hunting all over the house, and they were here all the time."

Mr. Benn stooped to pick up Algernon and Bobs, and Tabitha began to miaow sadly. "Come along, Tabitha", he said. And he and his wife left the clearing with the kittens, followed by a very miserable Tabitha.

"Well!" gasped Swisket, popping out of the hollow in the tree trunk. "Well well well well *well*!"

"Grumph", said Red Setter. He was hurt because the Grown-Ups hadn't noticed him, and the thought crossed his mind that perhaps the Grown-Ups were going to keep Tabitha's kittens: that would mean five cats in the house after all! He gave a little groan and lay down to think about the disadvantages of living in a house where there were *cats* ....

"What's happened?" asked Tomtit, waking up.

"The Grown-Ups have stolen Tabitha's kittens", Horace announced gravely.

"What?" muttered Oohoo, coming round from a deep sleep. "How disgraceful!" And he promptly fell fast asleep again.

"Poor Tabitha", said Swisket.

"Poor kittens!" said Horace, and the others nodded solemnly.

The next day, they all met again by the Old Oak Tree to talk about Tabitha's misfortune, and they were deep in conversation when Tabitha strolled into the clearing and seated herself by the stream.

"Hello, Tabitha dear", said Swisket gently.

"Poor Tabitha", murmured Oohoo sympathetically.

"Those dear, dear kittens!" sighed Horace.

"What on earth is all the fuss about?" asked Tabitha, calmly cleaning her whiskers.

Red Setter cocked his head to one side. "Don't you mind if the Grown-Ups take your kittens away?" he asked.

"Of course not!" snapped Tabitha.

"I thought you were frightened", said Oohoo in a puzzled voice.

"Me?" replied Tabitha. "Me, frightened?" She hissed with disgust. "I'm *never* frightened."

"What have the Grown-Ups done with your kittens?" asked Tomtit, very politely.

Tabitha stretched herself lazily and yawned. "Mirabelle has gone to live with the Jeffersons", she declared proudly. Mr. Jefferson was the owner of the Green Wood, so obviously Mirabelle was highly honoured. "Bobs has gone to the farm", Tabitha continued. "He'll make a very good farm cat, and he'll have plenty of fields to roam round in."

"What about Petrinella?" asked Swisket.

Tabitha beamed with delight. "Petrinella has gone to live with the doctor", she told them. "The doctor's wife said she had only seen one prettier cat, ever!"

"Who was that?" asked Red Setter.

"Me, of course", replied Tabitha impatiently. She thought the fact was so obvious that he needn't have asked.

"And what has happened to little Algernon?" asked Horace.

"He's going to live next door", said Tabitha with satisfaction. "I'll be able to keep an eye on him – he's not very strong."

"Your Grown-Ups have been quite sensible really, haven't they?" commented Oohoo. "I mean, considering what Grown-Ups are usually like …."

"Yes", agreed Tabitha, "but naturally, I knew what they were going to do all along."

Red Setter could hardly believe his ears. He remembered the terrified, shivering cat who had come to ask for their help a week ago – well, really, it was just too bad! She must have been pretending to be frightened!

Tabitha looked round severely. She could tell that the others did not quite believe what she had just said. "You forget", she said, slowly and deliberately, "you *all* forget that I am an extremely clever cat!" She gazed up into the branches of the Old Oak Tree, and her green eyes twinkled in the sunshine. "You see, I *understand* Grown-Ups", she purred. And then she stalked out of the clearing to see how Algernon was getting on in the house next door.

JÜRGEN DIETHE

PLACING THE SOUL

THE IMAGES ARE FADING.

The glass has seen
too much rain,
and the wind whips salt
against a surface
whose days of lustre
are retreating beyond our memory.

The images are fading.
I rub my eyes,
but no salt is blinding me,
and shapes and sizes
have begun to shift
and lose their meaning.

The images are fading.
Day by day, the memories
are building up,
and day by day
their structures buckle,
loose pieces clutter
a surface dull and brittle.

The images are fading
like pictures
left in the sun
and cast aside,
a lingering tear, perhaps,
but history will not be kind to them.

The images are fading.
Out there are hobnailed boots

trampling on the flowers,
and through a veil of tears,
the world recedes,
and pictures blur and crumble.

TRACES

Traces that keep my anxieties burning.
I see snow where sun should be scorching.
The hesitating steps of a robin.
What's happening behind its shiny breast?
Why the snow, forever the snow?

The white is blinding in the summer sun.
The pain coils round my eyeballs.
I seek relief in the white blanket
but find only dust, grating and sticky.
The robin, meanwhile, has died of thirst.

My garden, it carries a curse.
Where shall I look for the traces now
to feed my worries? In the flames
fanning a tsunami of headaches
I close my burning eyes and find calm.

There is that: a meeting-point of all traces.

DAYS OF HUBRIS

We touched the earth,
and the earth displayed her wounds.
She is bleeding black
where her children were torn from her.
See, she cries,
and floods fill the valleys,
cover the flats
and hide the deep scars.

Oh, what have we done
in the days of hubris,
when just playing games
was brutal punishment
for the greatest beauty
in all of the cosmos?

The cosmos neither knows nor cares,
time marches on
from the beginning
to a distant end
in a cold void
pockmarked by the corpses
of our world.

So does it matter
what we do to our earth?
Who else will know
of the beginning and the end?
Here is a moment
of the ultimate significance.

DORIAN GREY

When you visit people,
sneak up the stairs
and creep into the attic.
Feel your way under the rafters
where spider webs and dust motes gather.
There you find the greying pictures,
shaggy beards and thinning hair
and lines that furrow ever deeper.

Downstairs they chatter proudly
of the recipes that give eternal youth,
of superfoods, exotic treatments,
gyms and the benefits
of Nordic walking and expensive spas.
A good living for the artist
whose magic must be hidden
when time is to be stretched and faked.

Outside, the summer ends,
and reaping time has started.
Sit by the ripe and yellow field
and feel a chill in ageing bones.
How peaceful is the world!
Art is long, and life is short.

NO MAN'S LAND

Growing up is easier said than done.
Take my case:
I have come through a long life
of working and paying my dues,
punctually and conscientiously,
and here I am, among my peers,
and feel: they're the ones
with the world behind them
and the experience.

Do I genuflect,
do I display a complex of inferiority?
Or do they see me as what I am?

I wander around
as the youth that I was,
with the young knowing very well
that I am beyond the boundary.
The inner youth cannot reach out
into a wrinkled skin
and into slowing limbs.
Don't make yourself ridiculous
in this no man's land
between the timid soul
and the fading light.

DALI'S REVENGE

I never knew the cause,
but stories of melting clock faces
were puzzling beyond belief.
Had Salvador Dali risen
on a course to change the world?

Where would time go
when hands desperately
searched for numbers
and got entangled
in a sticky liquid?

Where would we go
when the lines between
yesterday and tomorrow
became smudged, burying
our present in their wet embrace?

So let us dance then,
watch the planets tumble
while the sun searches for his power,
night and day stop obeying
and the march of time is halted.

And our dance-steps
cease to have
a beginning
or an end.
Hold me while you can.

THE BALL

Come out and play, they shouted,
but the time was short,
and the ball was ending early.

There was hesitation in the dance-steps,
brains were clicking slowly,
and the painted faces started melting.

Why don't we swim, she whispered,
the lake is warm, the moon-light silver,
and toothed creatures will be all asleep now.

There was no wind that led the gowns to flutter,
like waves they surged to rise and fall,
stiff bonnets hiding glowing broken faces.

The midnight clock had long been silent.
Ghosts were everywhere in that morbid night.
But who could tell the spirit from the spectre?

One final kiss now to consume me.
At the end – was it hours? – lips were bony.
And the rising dawn surveyed a ghastly wreckage.

ROUND THE EDGES

Carefully,
I have danced round the edges.
The music was never very loud.
Who wants to be
the centre of attention?
My life has enough knowledge
to whisper caution
before I expose my ambition.

Oh, inside I can be strong.
For a moment at least.
But doubts are never far away.
Rivers run fast,
and stepping-stones
are full of treachery.
Always searching for bridges.

And thus, the other side is out of reach.
Oh, there are beautiful vistas,
the paths are splendid
and lead to further mountains,
green fields with many flowers.
While tears of frustration
turn the coward's side
into a dangerous morass.

And suddenly the music shrieks.
But no one feels like dancing.
Turn back and seek
the path into the valley.
And be careful

with the lying tales
of a heroic walk
deep into mysterious mountains.

The truth is rather different anyway.
On the other bank
were higher mountains,
and their soaring flanks
were pathless and too steep
for our hesitating hero,
who's now reduced to skirting
carefully
round the edges of another truth.

JUST WATCHING

The flash of a smile,
a menu of love
eagerly digested
and forgotten perhaps
in a matter of hours.

The array of bodies
is irresistible,
beaches palpitating
with stories of lust
and nightly fulfilment.

Some are just watching
across chasms of time
secretly knowing
of joyous conquests
and shattered hopes,
and the short spans at the table
where beautiful creations
die their natural deaths,
and the wine yields to a thirst
quite unquenchable and never fulfilled.

Then they go home,
nagged by disappointment
and images brightened
by a stream of forgetting.
Lucky those who just watch.
But still: something
is stirring inside
where memories are created.

DAYS OF BEAUTY

I look back to the days
when beauty
could flaunt itself
unashamed,
when virgins rose from the sea
in cascades
of pink waves,
when the sun was fresh
and even the dying hind
adorned the leaves
with a sprinkling
of innocent red.

You have grown wrinkles,
my dear, since then,
the mirror is cracked
and cannot speak
as to who the greatest beauty is.
Maybe she has long departed,
too sad for her
the slow decline
on the road to decay.

Not my memory,
not my own.
We adorn the tales
of a glorious past
and an innocence
that, too, was bathed in blood.

And yet: mirror, mirror on the wall,
who's the fairest of them all?
Who would think of such a question now?

There you are.
These feel like the latter days
when judgement is upon us,
and it will be harsh
under beauty's
steely gaze
and accusing finger.

PLACING THE SOUL

Had I not always known?
I was forever seeking mountains,
but sometimes forgot the sea.
Placing your soul
is taking life into your hand:
here I decide
where nature wills me.

Some speak of God.
But your soul knows better.
It will reside,
invisible and insubstantial
where you found your home.

The mountains and the sea
as close to immortality
as the ever-shifting earth
will ever get.

The sea will roll
until the sun has drunk it,
when only mountains
and their churning offspring
will remain.

There, in the beauty and the terror
of breaking, mourning rock,
re-birth and erosion
is a restless resting-place
for a soul
plagued by immortality.

LIGHT OF THE NIGHT

The light of the night
is my constant companion.
It broods over my chair.
It speaks of the hope
that the day might never end.

But it is long gone.
Illusions flourish
in the light of the night.
The passing of the days
becomes so blurred
it never happens.

Painless transition
until sleep finally
grabs hold of me
and leads me
through many worlds
to an awakening.

Not just another day,
finally, merely postponed,
but to a daily small recognition
that the light of the night
is a friend without power,

a master of illusion
through fleeting moments
only.

NOT INNOCENT

For I am not innocent.
There is still power in the ancient days.
Many lives speak accusations.
Rolling dice is no defence.
Why did I think
that walking in the woods
would free me from reality?

I can merely hope
that the old stories
would be kind to me,
that costly battles
would stay buried,
that walking by the sea
would give me pristine waves.

But there are echoes everywhere.
The knowing birds see who I am.
Flowers shiver in my shade,
and the voices raise their pitch.
Everything inside, I whisper,
as my hollow bones
creak and crack precariously.

I must ignore the voices.
Ancient foes arise in many ways.
No: innocent I'm not,
but there is virtue in my anger,
and for now and just
I vow to stay upright.

NEW YEARS

Expectations are always wrong,
hopes confounded,
good intentions defeated,
and let's not even start
about resolutions.

Why should a new year
be better than the old:
there lies an enemy defeated,
and here I am,
carrying my scars
into a new battle –

how long can I keep going?

My armour is going rusty,
the sword has lost its edge,
and every new opponent
is stronger than the last.

I want to lie down,
just for a while,
breathe easy
and think about my options.

You fool –
tomorrow will keep coming,
and soon, victoriously.

TOO QUICKLY

For me, the day came far too quickly.
But, I said, I am not ready,
in an anxious repetition
of a cliché to end all clichés.

There was a hollow laughter.
No one's ready, no one ever,
as I knew far too well.
And the voice was dripping with contempt.

So I left my gorgeous valley,
climbed a stony path
that promised much
of days among the gods.

There was no promise there.
All around, the mountains rose in threat.
The path, not chosen but dictated,
sapped the little strength there was.

But still it rose, ever steeper,
and the peaks around
remained remote, cold and stern,
raising hoary heads ever higher.

Night came in the broken light
of another world all new to me,
but I knew where I was headed
in a cruel landscape just for me.

O yes, I was ready after all,

in a shattered desert
crawling now on hands and knees
as pain gripped breaking flesh and bone.

Into a land of utter stillness,
beautifully lit by lakes of fire,
and only deep inside
a murmur rose, then tailing off

mercifully into nothing,
as the breaking eyes
saw finally
what they had come for.

CALL ME TOMORROW

when I might be in
tending the curtains
and preparing the carpets
for the next dance
they might have to carry.

Call me tomorrow
and I might give you some time
between sweeping the floor
and arranging flowers
to hide the cracks
criss-crossing the walls.

Call me tomorrow
when I shall have risen
from the small death
of a night's sleep
and am frantically
dusting trinkets and cups.

Call me tomorrow
when I speak to the spiders
and cajole flies in their webs
and stare at hollow windows
where broken glass
lets the wind in.

Call me tomorrow
when my abandoned life
still wanders through the wreckage

but has stopped minding
lost years and lost chances
and, above all, a lost mind.

FOR A DAY

The light is fading.
Night is drawing in.
I thought there would be joy
in the last hours,
but only the sad knowledge
of a day that was wasted.

There is the metaphor.
Some creatures live
just for a day,
some for years into darkness.
Who is the happier,
I wonder?

AFTER ALL A TRAGEDY

At the end of this sleep
there is a dream of no return –
where does it go,
when does it end?

Does this dream know
of its own end
when all the switches
turn to zero?

Maybe all those minutes
are all black –
but whom do I fool?
What a lovely story:
died peacefully
in their sleep.

Is a paradise
that was lost on the journey
to be regained in those moments?
Or just a point of light,
and then it's gone.

Fear not the millennia
you will never see.
No different to millennia
you have never seen.

A small window, nothing more
into the history of our universe,
it opens and it shuts

and only some of us
have the courage to look out.

But there's the tragedy:
all the striving,
all the thinking,
lost in the decay,
and only some
precariously exist
for a little longer
in printed symbols
slowly fading
bound in rotting covers.

QUIET MOMENTS

when I wonder
where I go.
When I wonder
how long I'll go.

Quiet moments
when at least
time seems to stop.
When illusions
serve to comfort.

Quiet moments
when my life
feels in balance.
When all meanders
find direction.

Quiet moments
when the daily fear
is suspended.
When my busy mind
just empties, for a moment.

Quiet moments,
alas, are not to last,
crowds always waiting.

When I drifted from the question
where and for how long,
I tried to shut the door,
but others have a key,

and it keeps turning,
after the glory
of a quiet moment.

MARGINS

We have extended the limits,
and now we are searching
at the margins
of a world
that grows and shrinks
with the seasons.
Now it is very small,
and there are many secrets
in the dark just beyond
the shortened horizon.

After the fireworks
of the sunset
we turn to each other
feeling for the late glow
being swallowed by the night
and seek the warmth
we might be privileged to find.

Now it is winter.
Now the nights are long,
but the magic is still there,
deeply hidden,
waiting to be woken
in the revolution
of the age-old cycle.

Let us redraw the margins.
There was wisdom
in adapting, in accommodating
to the turning of the wheel.

STORM

The houses by the water are mostly blind.
Hardly a soul ventures out into the wind.
Waiters tend to rare fugitives
from their lonely confinement.
Boats moan on their anchors.
Rubbish bobs on the trembling water.
Now and then, an engine breaks the howling,
locals in their homes breathe relief.
Raucous gales push through empty streets.
Outside, angry waves are crashing,
eternal rocks continuing their slow decay.
Those who need to sort their painted faces,
hope and fear mingling in new final statements.

HEBRIDEAN MOMENTS

Under the wind,
out in the west,
there is magic.
White sand,
washed daily
by the sea
and the rain.
Clouds rush in,
break and scatter
cut by a sudden
shallow sun.
Grass breathing deeply
ducking under hardened feet
in the daily rush
of the seasons.
Wings piercing air
trained in the fallacy
and beauty
of the moment.
The power of the sea
sometimes forgotten
in the glittering calm.
Under the surface
life goes on
even when land
ducks against
towering breakers.
You become tolerant here
at the edge of the void,
seek shelter
when it opens
and caress the time
when it is happy.

GLIMPSE

Stunned by the overwhelming wisdom
of the flower in bloom,
by the eternal vigilance
of the bee
and her graceful dances
telling of secret places,

the predatory spirit and intelligence
of the sharp-hunting bird,
the wily skills
of the humble cat
that knows nothing of humility.

I admire the grass,
lowliest of plants
and yet the great creator
in its never-ending sacrifice.

Great circles everywhere,
only some contribute nothing,
and take and take and take.

As I stand and observe
I glimpse of the knowledge
and shudder in a sudden chill
and know which is my end
of the spectrum.

SPEAKING OF WINTER

It is cold out there, my dear,
the rain has fallen,
has turned to ice,
sharp spears on an earth
that's full of wounds,
defeats, nothing but defeats.

Tortured by the sun,
waterboarded by the rain,
pierced when frost sets off
on its last campaign,
helplessness
camouflaged by brutality.

You don't know this yet, my dear,
just dim awareness
safely locked
in a suit of hope
that fits so badly.

But you and me,
we huddle under garments
and speak of winter,
without irony
and with just a touch
of guilt.

ROBIN

The red-breasted one
has danced undaunted,
skipping around feet,
promiscuous in his affection –

o little robin,
how grateful you should be
that no cat's in residence!

And the tough days ahead
are no dancing matter –
are you prepared,
little robin?

Christmas relies on you,
but you are lonely,
and the pretty snow
is a poor companion.

Well, maybe not.
Skipping with beady eyes –
someone gives thanks
for global warming.

FRAGILE WORLD

When the astronauts
looked back to the earth,
they saw it was fragile.
From the grey deserts of the moon
the earth was a magic apparition
gleaming in the colour of life
oh so small
against a blackness
deeper than any abyss
and as cold as the atoms will allow.

And all alone.
Under the thin haze
over her fuzzy edge
nothing is ever alone
however lonely
we go to bed at night
and wake up in the morning.

Many things are fragile here
in a world stoically
surviving every disaster.
Not immortal:
what would the rocks do
if they knew
that they will melt
in the final sun-storm?

They would grow
and be crushed,
be washed to the sea

and rise again
in patient majesty
as they have done
since the earth was young,
congealed from primeval fire.

There is memory
in the atoms,
here and on the moon,
memory of greater fires,
mighty furnaces
before they found their destiny.

For ever and ever
into an endless future
cold and dark
beyond measure,
now truly lonely
and fragile no more.

REMEMBRANCE SUNDAY

They remind us.
From beyond the grave.
Only that graves
were a luxury
they were not granted.

Sometimes dogs have dug
and found rotting bones.
Slavering tongues recoiled in horror.
They smelt of history
rotten to the core
from ancient suffering.

Red poppies for that?
There, look at the heroes.
At the rictus of the skulls.
The braves and the cowards,
hurrah and hiding,
all in that jumble.

How false are the memories
we have learned
in the image of the plastic poppy?
Friend and enemy,
defence of freedom
and displays of hypocrisy.

Those are the rituals
of Remembrance Sundays.
The dead are tolerant and flexible,
bones are nothing,

carbon atoms drifting home.

And the warriors of today
ask awkwardly:
what is it all about?
We have seen the deaths
and the suffering,

of the innocent and the unarmed,
a tide of blood
flowing through humanity
from the dawn of a fatal race,
and war, always war
will burn the poppies.

HISTORY

Always there is blood at the end
when the grand events are recounted.
The fall of the leaders
is faithfully retold,
let us shudder
at their gruesome fates
when another rise
along a bloody path
has ended yet again in blood.

Who knows about the millions
whose innocence was never doubted,
who never wrote their lives in blood
but fed in their millions
the never-drying ocean of blood?

Desperate faces
illuminated
by the flames
of their houses.
Crying children
whose tears
were only dried
by the sword.
Endless humanity
in the maelstrom
of a senseless wave
of destruction.

But why speak of the past?
Human intelligence has never changed,

and how better to use it
than in games of power
with their endless butchery?

RICHARD III

If only he'd known,
some pride could have been rescued
in his final minutes.
Cut up on the field of battle,
his crown worthless
in the search for a horse.

Not much time for him
in the game of thrones
of fifteenth-century England
when the fate
of princes in the Tower
was but a trifle.

Having limped into history,
he cut a swathe
into short years
when a new order
flickered on the horizon,
but not for him, in the end,
nor was he the one
who wrote his history.

What came of that?
His friends now try to correct
Henry and William,
but first they have to wipe away
curtain after curtain
of a bloody life,

and who knows
whether the car park
was not more apt
than the cathedral.

DOWNFALL

Now the king has spoken,
saddened, as his house is broken,
and whisper as they say
when the plague holds sway:
we all fall down,
majesty, where is your crown?

The king goes hunting,
and we all wear bunting,
and the deer is sick
hearing the beater's stick,
and in the crashing night
death is the winner without fight.

The king has many friends,
but where are they when it ends?
Even he hears through the merry song
that they're plotting him a fearful wrong.
O yes, when the storm-clouds gather
life weighs no more than a feather.

BRAVE MAN

His hands shook almost imperceptibly.
He was a brave man.
But inside, the sweat of the soul
fell in torrents.
His heart of iron blunted
by a veneer of rust.
His legs and arms were moving,
but hinges screamed in protest.

This was not the tin-man.
Go and oil the armour,
but the sword is sharp,
and the rising flood
of bitter fear
has done nothing
but fuel the hatred.

Steel against skin,
iron against bones,
no competition as yet.

There the warriors
rumble through the streets –
who would have thought
that their leader
is dying of fear?

Their humanity in iron fetters.
They need wakening
to let the rain touch their hearts.
Then the army

will hesitate,
fall out of step,
eat a ration of doubt.

Then look at their hands.
Look at the muzzles
of their vicious guns.
Are they shaking
ever so slightly?

Let your courage
melt their brains of steel.
And hope that their souls
consume them
before a final act of defiance
launches firepower
mere human skin
is far too weak to resist.

On the empty plain
the rusty hulks
will lose their fear
and iron upon iron
will rust in bravery,
glinting steel waiting to be found
and admired.

We always knew
that hope was in vain.
The real bravery
merely flitting through the pages
of a book in a corner
of a long-forgotten library.

RAINY DAYS

My savings are too vulnerable.
Every time it rains
they decline –
why did I choose to save
for a rainy day?

What is a rainy day?
When it pours,
cascades in sheets,
is whipped by storms
driven from the west,
or does the manna
for the thirsting plants
wash away my money?
What about the steady trickle
of a drizzly shower?

Oh, you are so exposed.
Had I known about
the rainy days
I would have organised
wise investments,
a roof perhaps
to let my banknotes shelter –
even a simple sheet of plastic
would be preferable.

The rain is gnawing, melting,
and the damp is creeping
through the layers.
There are gaps already
that expose the bleak reality
of encroaching poverty.

DEADLY SINS

The seven deadly sins —
oh, they are harmless,
they serve to hide failings
that can never be forgiven.
And yet:
some are worse than others.

Ah, let them lust.
Let them ignore
the old bearded moralists
with their shrivelled minds
that have long forgotten
the glories of their bodies.
Humanity would have ended
long ago without this lust.

Gluttony is somewhat different.
This is not a game of zeros.
One man's gluttony
is another man's starvation —
or perhaps not quite that simple?
All right, let him have his pudding.

Greedy gut,
but now things get more serious.
Be suspicious when they say
that greed is good.
By itself, it never ends,
so make it harmless.
Such are innocuous words
for serious games of power.

Sloth, on the other hand,
is eminently lovable.
As it slowly creeps,
grip by grip,
and while you rest,
the world will pass
in harmless contemplation.

But do not speak to me
of wrath.
This is the privilege of gods.
There may be righteous anger,
but don't let them
lose their heads
all around you.
And yet: let them rage,
real deadly sins
are made in icy calm.

Where envy is just smiled upon.
O yes, this is a different green.
Not life-affirming.
But shouldn't one start thinking
about the source of envy?
Greed rewarded?
Sloth by unearned riches?
Envy may just have a point
and unintended benefits.

And when pride's a deadly sin
just take the opposite:
the sly aggression of humility

that is more sinful pride
than standing up
and speaking out against the wrongs.

O yes, there are those deadly sins.
They leave victims in their wake,
are drenched in blood,
kill the future of the world,
laugh in the face of what is real,
because power will subsist,
and no one reaps the harvest:
that is for the innocent who follow.

DREAMSCAPES – TWO STORIES

THE DREAM

He had sunk into a particularly dark dream. His dreams were always threatening, full of dangers, turbulence and violence. Wars, fires, earthquakes raged around him, he plunged into accidents, his house fell apart, sometimes he was threatened by dark, perhaps archetypal forces, like birds attacking him around his windows. At other times, his dreams were almost harmless, like the classic manifestations of helplessness, like not being able to run away, because the legs would not work or were too heavy, or finding himself naked in public. We all know those. And there were, very occasionally, almost blissful moments when the loves he never had and had never known meandered through his subconscious and he wavered, almost knowingly, between his present and his agonised younger self.

But whatever they were, they were always oddly comforting. After all, he never died in his dreams. Whatever happened around him, no matter what frustration plagued him, he always came out of it unscathed. Even when a gang once beat him up, there was no pain, and there was no injury. So he didn't mind, especially as it was a really nice feeling to wake up and be rid of the dark forces of his sleep. And anyway, he often had only a very vague recollection of the journeys undertaken by his subconscious self. There was a vague curiosity as to what they might mean, and if his brain was just tidying up the clutter of the day: where did the images come from, images largely unknown or unseen?

Tonight, however, his dream was different. He had always been the victim of whatever occurred around him, but tonight he seemed to act. And how. He stepped out of his flat and the house, he seemed to see the scene quite clearly, because there were people in the street, people he knew although but vaguely. He never talked much to the neighbours, he was proud of being very self-contained. Anyway, these people suddenly succumbed to him, fell to the ground, bleeding from stab-wounds. Then he noticed the large kitchen knife in his hand, smeared with blood. And when he looked up, suddenly the whole row of houses on the opposite side of the street was ablaze, people crying for help, stumbling out of front doors, climbing through windows. And then they fell, clutching those terrible wounds, and his arm suddenly felt so very tired. Why don't they defend themselves, he thought to himself, but no, all they did was stumble forward and fall, anyone, men, women, children, the whole street seemed to be a killing field, and he alone upright in the middle, with a tired arm and a bloody kitchen knife.

What happened next was that he woke up, with a start, bathed in sweat. Never had he had such a dream. This time, there was real fear. It was still very early in the morning, but it was summer, and there was already some light, although the sun was still below the horizon. But there was his flat, there were the walls, and there was the window to the street. He stumbled to the window, opened the curtain and looked at a blackened wall opposite. He turned left and right, all the houses on the other side looked gutted or badly damaged from what must have been a huge fire. Why had he slept through such a calamity? Why had he heard no fire engines, no cries for help, no breaking timbers and crashing tiles? Just an eerie silence, and then he looked down to the street, and there they were, bodies, contorted, bloody, with gaping wounds, just about visible in the early light of morning. Quickly, he drew the curtain again, and then, suddenly, black enveloped his mind.

He held the bloody knife, but the interrogator was already there, staring at him. Nothing else at first. He began to talk, explained it had only been a dream, how could these things have happened, he had no idea, there was no rhyme or reason. Then the interrogator began to beat him, his fist landed in his face repeatedly, he felt his nose break, blood ran over his eyes, and then he fell off the chair down to the concrete floor. And everything was black again.

He woke up, in his bed. How much later was it? What was it like outside? But he saw no light, it seemed to be dark on the other side of his curtain. And then he felt the excruciating pain in his head. He touched it gingerly, felt congealed blood, he touched his nose, it hurt like hell, and it seemed to be all loose . . . Carefully he got up, went to the bathroom and looked in the mirror. His face was an absolute mess. Where had he been? With a rising feeling of panic, he went to the window, opened the curtain. The streetlights were on, it was obviously night, and there seemed to be nothing wrong with the houses opposite. The street was absolutely deserted, except for a large kitchen knife glistening on the pavement. And then the world faded away again.

Now he found himself in a prison cell. That, too, seemed strange. His injuries had gone, but it was cold and uncomfortable. A bucket in the corner. A hard bed. A shelf. A small chest of drawers, a hand-basin in the other corner. Nothing else. Barred windows with profound darkness on the other side. There was almost a feeling of relief creeping through his dream, or so he tried to tell himself. But then he noticed the silence. Aren't dreams supposed to be silent? Who remembers? Well, it was night, after all, but when a grey light crept across his prison bars and the silence seemed to deepen, it occurred to him that there were no voices anywhere, no rushing feet, the whole prison seemed to be deserted. Or was there just his cell and nothing else? The sense of panic returned. He woke up with a start – here, too, total silence awaited him. He went to his window to greet the daylight on the other side of his curtain – but when he opened it, there was no street any more, no houses opposite, just nothing, a void – wherever he looked, there seemed to be a grey mist, swallowing sounds and sights and then even his window. He returned to the comfort of darkness, now profoundly dreamless.

THE FOREST

They were wonderful trees – tall, imposing, almost eerie in their regular growth, as if someone had guarded them from their youth making sure that the distribution of their branches corresponded to some ideal type tree. While he walked past them, he harboured thoughts of Plato and ghostly worlds of ideas that ruled physical beings. Silly, really. But while still walking through the fields, he had seen this forest in the distance and felt attracted by the dark-green foliage, and when he finally entered it, still on a well-marked path, it felt almost like walking into a cathedral. This was not a forest with dense undergrowth, on the contrary, the trees were well-spaced and therefore able to unfold their branches without being hindered by encroaching neighbours. He liked forests, anyway, being German, it felt quite natural. It was a bit pompous to say that the German soul had a natural affinity to the forest – what a horrendous cliché – but when you're actually there, it doesn't feel quite so far-fetched. Because the trees were so well-spaced, there was also generous vegetation on the forest floor, and with it being late summer, the first of the autumn's fungi had begun to rear their heads. He felt tempted to pick some of those he was familiar with, but, of course, there was no point, what was he going to do with them?

After all, he was quite a long way from home. He had been careless – a bus journey into the country, and then he had just set off walking without really thinking how to get back. He was not too worried: on the way out he had passed a country inn which he surely would be able to find again, if all else failed and there was no transport back. There were quite a few hours of daylight left, and the weather was fine and settled. So he continued on his way deeper into the woods, which he assumed to stretch maybe for a few miles, before opening up to fields again. He had a vague memory from looking at a map, although he had actually never travelled in this direction. He was slightly surprised that he encountered no one else on his walk, but it was a weekday, and so he assumed that the general population was far too busy for a leisurely amble, and non-working parents with their children or pensioners would never get this far. He himself had taken a few days off from his office job, which was stiflingly boring. Being here in this serene place made him think that perhaps a career change might be in order. Although he didn't really have any clear idea in which direction that should take him.

Talking of direction: being deep in thought, he hadn't really noticed that the character of the wood was gradually changing, and the path he was on had begun to grow fainter. The wood was clearly getting denser and while not directly unpleasant, certainly more mysterious. The dappled sunlight on the grass had disappeared, as had the grass itself to a large degree – it was darker and noticeably cooler. I'll go just a little further, he thought to himself, maybe I'll get to the other end.

But there was no end in sight. The tree cover had become so dense that he couldn't have seen much anyway, and walking became a bit of an effort. He decided it was time to turn round, but now something really strange happened. He had still been walking on a path talking him through the remaining undergrowth and past the dead lower branches in what now had become a conifer forest, mainly spruce trees, he thought. But when he turned round, there was no path. He went a few steps further forward, turned round, and the path he had quite clearly been on had also disappeared. He looked at an almost impenetrable thicket, and the light had become very gloomy. Furthermore, he had now reached the foot of a fairly steep hill, which, as far as he could see, climbed at least two, three hundred feet. Which was also strange, because before he entered the woods, the landscape had appeared completely flat. No sign of any hills.

He decided that he might as well struggle up the slope, helped by the still continuing path, which climbed up at a slightly easier angle (and kept disappearing behind him, as he kept glancing back). But perhaps he could get a better view from the top. It took him about half an hour's climbing to reach a kind of rounded ridge – he must have ascended about 500 feet in that time. The ridge was still covered fairly densely by trees, but there were some rocky outcrops, one of them sufficiently tall to get above the tree tops. After a slightly awkward climb – he was a little worried about getting down again which is always scarier than going up – he plunged straight into the next surprise. He got a good view, but not the one he was expecting. There was no end to the forest whichever way he turned. What on earth was going on? He checked his watch – less than an hour-and-a-half had passed since he entered into the cathedral-like outer reaches of the forest. Which means, he could not have gone much further than about three miles. Now he was getting seriously worried. Where was his world? Not only did the tree cover stretch further than he could see, the whole landscape had changed. Where he remembered walking on flat forest floor, suddenly there was hill after hill, the whole landscape was a wave-like succession of peaks and troughs.

It became clear to him that he would be out here during the coming night, which was bad enough – he was going to be cold and hungry, and his first priority had to be contacting the (his?) world. So, he got his mobile phone out, just charged before he set off. But he had a bad feeling, and that was confirmed almost immediately: no signal, none whatsoever. All of a sudden, it became conceivable that he might actually die out here. But he had no idea what to do and where to go. So he sat down on a piece of dry ground, leaning against a rock. And fell asleep, almost immediately. How strange was that? He had not really been tired.

When he woke up again, he could feel that the sun was close to setting. Something was bothering him – a huge fly was exploring his face, it was at least two inches long. He waved his arm and it buzzed off, but what on earth was that? And the grass around him had also grown to a prodigious height, taller than him, in fact. Above his head dangled a blackberry, and that was nearly as big as his head, just out of reach. But when he stepped – naked – out of his clothes, which lay around him, he realised that it wasn't everything else that had become much bigger – he had become tiny. The same proportions but no taller than maybe seven, eight inches. I must be just a tenth of my original height, he calculated, frantically. He threw himself down and closed his eyes. When he opened them again a few seconds later, nothing had changed. He was naked and tiny, and now a giant ant was getting interested. He also managed to get rid of that, when he saw a squirrel hugging one of the enormous trees – it was considerably bigger than him. Lucky that squirrels are strictly vegetarian, unlike quite a few other inhabitants of the forest.

He looked round, desperate. He tried to remember, but his memory failed him, because with his body his brain had also shrunk. Without knowing, he was now at the level of the creatures of the forest, but nowhere near as well equipped. At least, a few pieces of fruit would be enough to still his hunger – if he could get them. With some effort he managed to reach a blackberry, which provided a lot of food, albeit messily. Not that he cared any more. But he felt the cold, and as it got dark under the trees he crawled into his clothes which provided warmth and comfort. And he dreamt of trees and ants and flies. His former life was now beyond his horizon.

Dimly he still hoped that all this was a dream in a dream, and he would wake up in a bed in a now distant life, but no such luck. As he struggled out of the shelter of his clothes, he realised dimly that the world was different yet again. The grass was even taller. He now had shrunk to a size of no more than two inches. He waded waste-high through dead leaves on the forest floor, noticed creatures he would have normally stepped upon. He struggled on for a few yards, which took all his energy, when he stood in front of a huge mountain with many small holes, covered thickly by pine needles. It was an ant hill.

And the ants came out, streams of them, surrounded him without touching. But it was as though they were guiding him to their home until he stood right in front of it. Then they took him. Grabbed him by the arms, legs, head and dragged him into one of the holes, which for some reason was large enough to fit through. As though they had known he would come. He was not hurt, but he could not resist, and it was very, very dark. The further he slipped inside, the warmer it became, but so dark, so dark, until they seemed to reach a large cavern, and strangely enough, there he could see, even if only dimly. The queen lay there, a vast, bloated body, almost as big as he was, pale white and laying eggs, constantly laying eggs while being tended by worker ants – others carried the eggs away to become more ants.

The ants that had brought him into this chamber, backed off now. He sat alone in front of the queen, and as his now tiny brain ticked over, he felt that he was losing all will power. He felt the queen speaking to him, although there was total silence except for the rustling of constantly moving worker ants that surrounded the queen. He himself also had no speech any more, there was only the insistent whisper in his brain from the motionless queen. Until there was nothing else there. He was told he was here to be sacrificed. His glance was directed into a corner of the room. There was a pile of tiny bones, and just one thought crept into his now miniscule brain: this forest had never been real, it was an artefact of a superior intelligence capable of manipulating human life. Then it switched off. Who knows what the purpose was of this sacrifice? Did human sacrifices ever have any purpose? He did not resist or move when sharp jaws cut up his body, despite the horrendous pain he was still capable of feeling, and switched off gratefully.

They found a pile of clothes in a field outside a stand of trees. His wallet and his phone served to identify a missing person, reported a few days previously. It was no more than a few hundred yards from the nearest bus stop. There was no hotel there, and there were certainly no hills in a flat landscape. Strangely enough, the clothes were crawling with ants.